I'M THE
BIGGEST!
IN THE # MOUNTAINS

LAURA K. MURRAY

CREATIVE EDUCATION   CREATIVE PAPERBACKS

CONT

ENTS

LET'S EXPLORE THE MOUNTAINS!

The air is dry and windy. Use your binoculars to search the rocky mountainside. Two bighorn sheep run toward each other. They crash their heavy horns together.

From Base to Summit

Mountain surroundings change as **elevation** increases. Temperatures drop. Snow falls. The alpine zone lies between the **snow line** and the **tree line**. Lower mountain zones have forests, lakes, and meadows.

elevation - height above sea level

snow line - the elevation above which year-round snow and ice cover begins

tree line - the elevation above which trees stop growing

Hawaii's Mauna Kea volcano (opposite) is the tallest mountain on Earth. From base to **summit**, it is taller than Mount Everest! But much of Mauna Kea is underwater.

Mt. Everest
29,029 ft (8,848 m)

Mauna Kea
13,796 ft (4,205 m) above sea level

19,685 ft (6,000 m) below sea level

sea level

summit - the highest point of a mountain

Surviving the Mountain

Trees with needle-shaped leaves are called conifers. Their narrow needles shed snow. Conifers such as the limber pine tree (below) have flexible branches. This helps them withstand strong winds.

High in the alpine zone, plants grow close to the ground. Many alpine wildflowers are **perennials**. Few plants that live for only a year grow here. Plants cannot grow above the snow line. This cold, windy zone is covered with ice and snow.

Animals, Big and Small

Bighorn sheep are some of the biggest animals in the alpine zone. Males, called rams, can weigh more than 300 pounds (136 kg). Their curved horns may be as heavy as 30 pounds (13.6 kg). Most bighorn sheep move to lower elevations for winter.

size comparison

size comparison

Andean condors are big, heavy birds. Their wings measure 10 feet (3 m) from tip to tip. Alpine bumblebees are much smaller. The queen spends winter underground. The rest of her colony dies.

Full of Life

From alpine bumblebees to bighorn sheep, mountains are full of life. What other amazing things can you discover about these high, rocky places?

Andean condor

alpine bumblebee

bighorn sheep

mountain goat

snowshoe hare

IN THE
MOUNTAINS

Highest summit on each continent:

7

Mount Kosciuszko
7,310 feet

6

Mount Vinson
16,050 feet

5

Mount Elbrus
18,510 feet

4

Kilimanjaro
19,341 feet

3

Denali
20,310 feet

2

Aconcagua
22,837 feet

1

Mount Everest
29,029 feet

Word Review

Do you remember what these words mean? Look at the pictures for clues, and go back to the page where the words were defined, if you need help.

colony page 17

elevation page 7

perennials page 13

snow line page 7

summit page 8

tree line page 7